Accessible Reading edition

MARVEL

FIGHT OR FLIGHT

This dyslexia-friendly edition uses:

- Fonts that can make it easier to distinguish between similar letters
- Uncomplicated layouts and spacing to stop the pages from being overcrowded
- Paper with a gentle tint that can help to reduce visual stress

Australian Dyslexia Association
Solutions for those who learn differently.

This book has been created in collaboration with the Australian Dyslexia Association.

Published by Scholastic Australia in 2022.
Scholastic Australia Pty Limited
PO Box 579 Gosford NSW 2250
ABN 11 000 614 577
www.scholastic.com.au

Part of the Scholastic Group
Sydney • Auckland • New York • Toronto • London • Mexico City • New Delhi • Hong Kong • Buenos Aires • Puerto Rico

ISBN 978-1-76120-402-9

Printed by McPherson's Printing Group, Maryborough, VIC.

MIX
Paper from responsible sources
FSC® C001695

Scholastic Australia's policy, in association with McPherson's Printing Group, is to use papers that are renewable and made efficiently from wood grown in responsibly managed forests, so as to minimise its environmental footprint.

10 9 8 7 6 5 4 3 2 1 22 23 24 25 26 / 2

Accessible Reading edition

MARVEL

FIGHT OR FLIGHT

STARRING

FALCON

By Chris 'Doc' Wyatt

Illustrated by
Tom Grummett, Drew Geraci
and Andy Troy

SCHOLASTIC
SYDNEY AUCKLAND NEW YORK TORONTO LONDON MEXICO CITY
NEW DELHI HONG KONG BUENOS AIRES PUERTO RICO

Featuring your favourites!

Falcon

Sam Wilson

Captain America

Iron Man

Hulk

Thor

Hawkeye

Black Widow

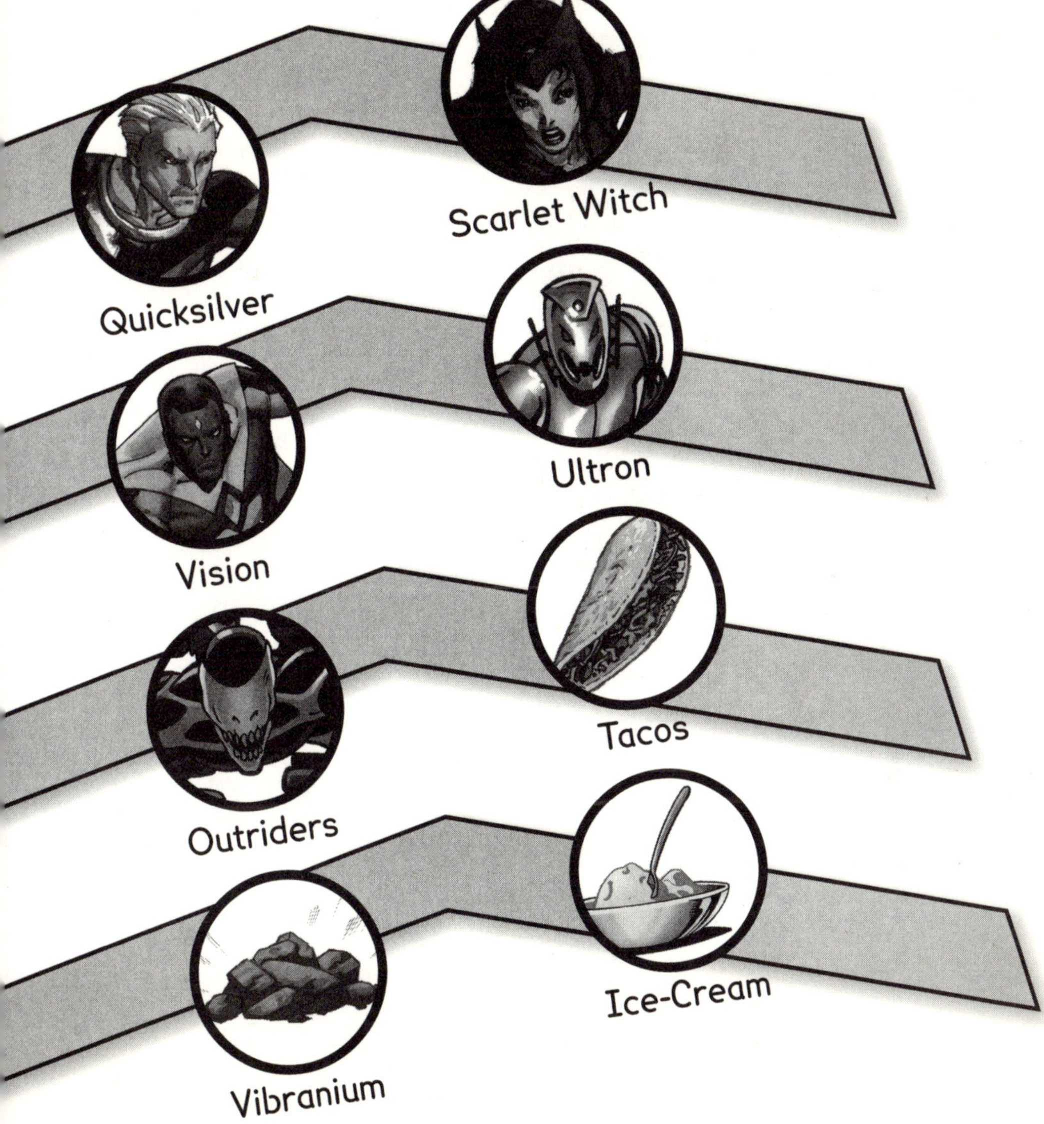
Scarlet Witch
Quicksilver
Ultron
Vision
Tacos
Outriders
Ice-Cream
Vibranium

The Story of Falcon

There came a day unlike any other, when Earth's Mightiest Heroes were united against a common threat. On that day, the Avengers were born, and **Sam Wilson** was their biggest fan. While still in school, Sam followed every one of the Avengers' battles by watching them on TV and reading about them online.

Sam dreamed that one day he, too, could be an Avenger . . . But how could he?

He wasn't a great hero, and he didn't have super powers. However, Sam was extremely smart, and he knew how to work hard. He excelled at his studies, and he spent all his spare time inventing new machines.

While still just a teenager, Sam Wilson found himself trapped with Captain America on a tropical island run by the villainous Red Skull. After a long battle, the two escaped, but barely. Cap was so impressed with Sam's skills, he suggested Sam train with him. Sam was accepted to the **S.H.I.E.L.D.** training program, and the two trained together and soon became best friends.

During his time at **S.H.I.E.L.D.**, Sam created an amazing invention—a personal wing-suit that gave him the power of flight at high speed. Wearing that suit on dangerous missions earned Sam the code name **Falcon**.

One day, after an adventure as Falcon, Sam came back to headquarters to find **Tony Stark**, the Avenger known as **Iron Man**, waiting for him. Tony explained that the **Avengers** were adding a few new members to their team . . . Would Sam be interested in joining?

Join the team that he'd loved since he was a boy? Become an Avenger, one of Earth's Mightiest Heroes?

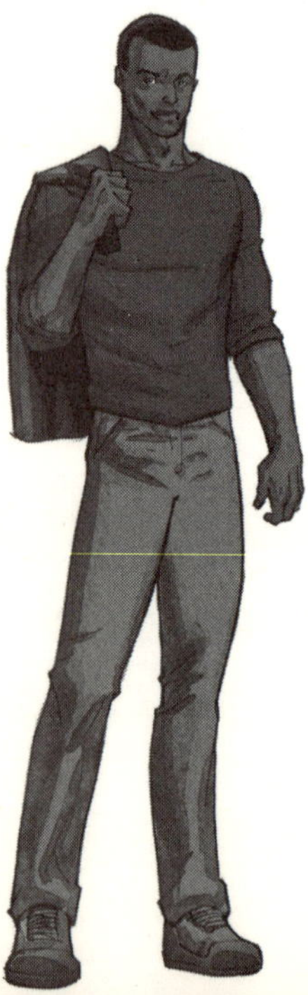

Oh, yeah, Sam was definitely interested. In fact, it was the best day of his life!

chapter 1

A gentle breeze rippled through the forest of tall, majestic redwoods. From where he sat positioned in the crook of a thick branch at the top of one of the trees, **Sam Wilson**, the Avenger known as **Falcon**, could see the forest all around him. It was a fantastic view, but he wasn't really enjoying it, because there was only one thing he was interested in . . .

Using the heads-up display in his costume's visor, Sam zoomed his vision in on something in one of the other trees. Someone just casually walking through the forest would never have spotted it; it was so well camouflaged—but Sam could see it.

It was a small wooden platform, built into the tree trunk, behind some branches.

On that platform was the one thing that Falcon most wanted in the world right then . . . **a small Blue flag.**

Falcon scanned the area. There was no sign of his opponent. No sound, either. He smiled to himself. Finally, after all this time, success was going to be his.

Sam whispered into the Avengers '**comm**', or communications unit, in his ear, signalling two **S.H.I.E.L.D.** agents who were assigned to his team. 'Okay,' said Falcon. 'It's go time. Converge on the target in **three . . . two . . . one . . . NOW!**'

Falcon suddenly leapt out from his tree, spreading out his wings, which let him fly across the forest towards his target. At the same time, the two **S.H.I.E.L.D.** agents leapt from their hiding places on the ground.

All three figures moved quickly, but fastest of all was Falcon. Hours and hours of practice with the wing-suit gave him surprising speed and manoeuvrability.

Within seconds, Falcon could see the flag in front of him. All he had to do was reach out and . . .

Falcon got slammed in the side so suddenly that it knocked the breath out of him! Someone had jumped out of a hiding place and tackled him in midair.

But it wasn't just 'someone'. It was none other than **Captain America!** Falcon tried to push Cap off him, but Cap held firm! With all the added weight, Falcon dropped out of the sky! He and Cap were still grappling when they landed in a barrel roll on the ground.

'**Fancy running into you here,**' joked Cap as he sprang back to his feet and hurled his famous shield. Cap's shield bounced around the forest, ricocheting off of some trees, before first taking down one **S.H.I.E.L.D.** agent, then the other. Falcon barely had time to rise to his feet before Cap had him covered again. Cap's shield landed effortlessly back in his hands.

'Well, Sam, what do you say?' asked Cap, a smile on his face.

'Yeah, you win, Cap,' Falcon admitted, his shoulders drooping.

'Don't feel bad,' Cap said, throwing an arm around his friend. 'No-one's ever beaten me in a "capture the flag" training exercise.'

'I'll be the first,' admitted Sam. 'Jarvis, end the program.'

'Yes, sir,' came a disembodied computer voice out of the sky as the whole forest–the trees, the ground, even the two **S.H.I.E.L.D.** agents–suddenly shimmered and then disappeared. All that could be seen now were the drab walls of the Avengers Tower's training room.

The whole thing had been a simulation, run by Jarvis, the Avengers Tower's computer system!

Cap and Falcon walked through a now-visible door and out into the hallway, as Cap said to Falcon, 'You're really coming along. You got very close, and also, having the two simulated **S.H.I.E.L.D.** agents on your team makes it a leadership exercise, so–'

Falcon didn't get to hear the end of Cap's thought, because Iron Man interrupted, racing down the hallway towards them. 'Cap! Sam!' Iron Man shouted urgently. 'Come with me right now. It's an

EMERGENCY!'

'What is it now?' asked Sam. 'Did Thor and Hulk get into another fight over who ate the last container of ice-cream?'

'Worse, much worse,' Iron Man said gravely. 'Hurry and see!'

Cap and Sam didn't miss another beat. They took off running after Iron Man.

chapter 2

Sam and Cap raced after Iron Man, following him into his lab. It was a place Sam knew well, having spent hundreds of hours working there on various inventions. His talent for dreaming up new technology was one of the reasons that Sam had wanted to become an Avenger.

One day, Sam had been aboard the **S.H.I.E.L.D.** Helicarrier when Tony Stark, the man inside the Iron Man armour, had walked right up to him.

'They tell me your name is Sam,' Tony had said. **'I want to talk to you about those wings of yours.'**

Stark had been so impressed with the wing-pack, as well as Sam's other inventions,

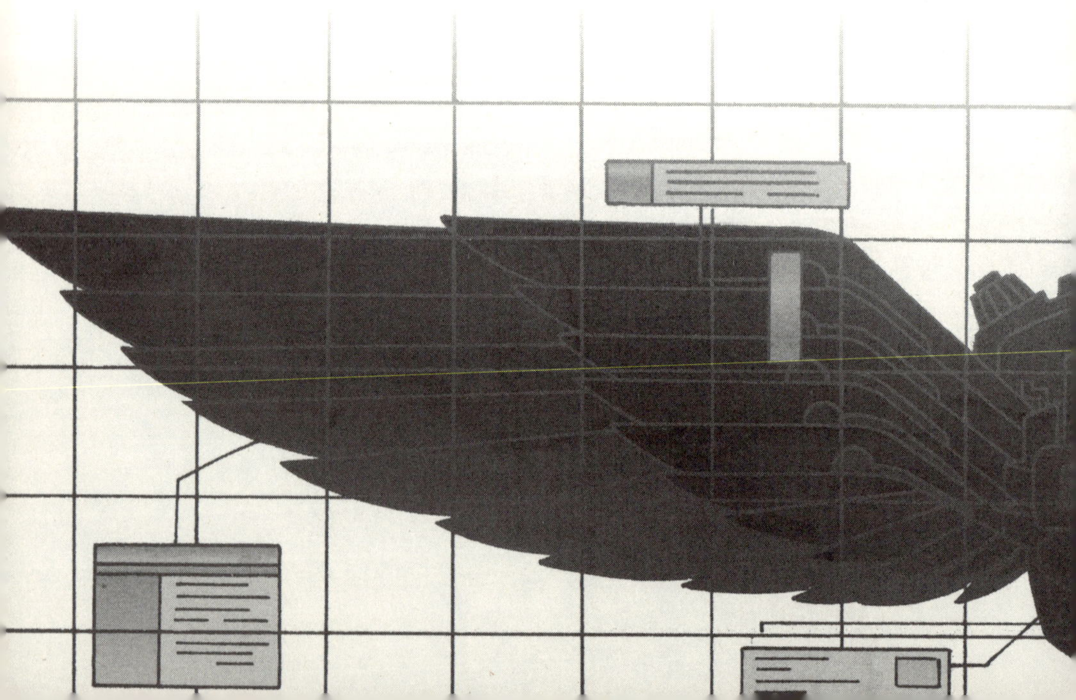

that he had invited Sam to come meet with the other Avengers.

Now Sam was eager to find out what this emergency was. If it had the usually unflappable Iron Man this upset, then it must be something serious, Sam thought.

'What happened?' asked Hulk, who was already standing in the lab with Thor when Cap, Iron Man and Sam arrived.

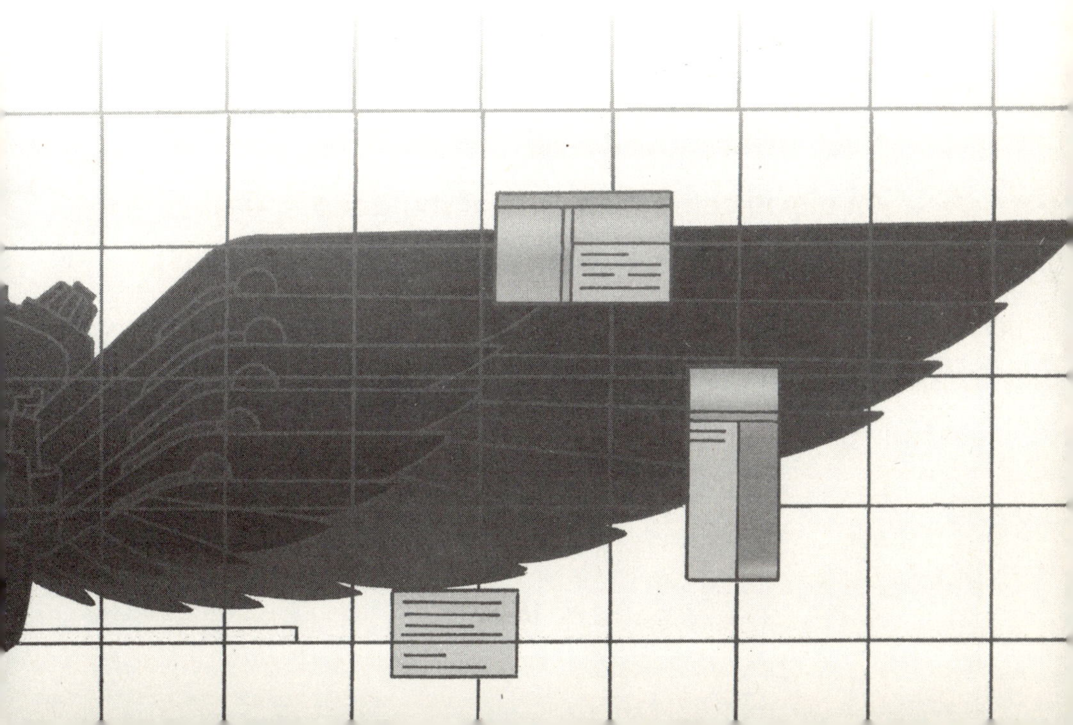

'Yes, Stark, why the alarm?' asked Thor. **'I was about to beat Hulk at a game of truck tossing.'**

'Beat HULK? Dream on, blondie,' sneered Hulk.

'An alarm came from one of my deep-space probes that . . .' Iron Man started, then trailed off. 'Wait. Did you say "truck tossing"? Where did you get the trucks? You haven't been down in the Stark Industries garage again, have you?'

Hulk and Thor quickly looked down, avoiding Iron Man's glare. 'Well . . . the thing is . . .' said Thor, sounding guilty.

'**Focus**,' Cap interrupted. 'Tony, what's this emergency?'

Iron Man remembered why they were all there. **'The probe picked up interstellar chatter indicating that . . . Thanos is back.'**

The air in the room was heavy. Thanos was an intergalactic alien warlord of incredible strength whom the team had tangled with before.

The last time they had met Thanos, the Avengers had saved Earth from his plans for its destruction . . . but only barely. If Thanos came back with an army . . . well, it was **unthinkable!**

'According to the chatter, Thanos is amassing an army of Outriders just outside the orbit of Pluto. Once his invasion fleet is fully assembled, he intends to attack!' continued Iron Man. 'We have to go check this trouble out . . .

NOW!'

Iron Man pointed to Cap, Hulk and Thor as he said, **'It should be the four of us to go. Sam can stay here and mind the fort with the others.'**

The whole team agreed.

A few minutes later, Sam watched as Iron Man, Cap, Hulk and Thor loaded into one of the **Quinjets** and prepared for launch into space.

'What do I do while you're gone?' Sam asked Cap as he headed up the ship's ramp.

'You do what you think is best. The others will look to you for leadership,' Cap said, referring to the members of the Avengers who weren't going on the space mission. 'With us gone, you're in charge, Sam,' Cap concluded as the ship's door shut between them.

In charge . . . Sam thought as he watched the Quinjet disappear into the atmosphere, bound for outer space.

I'M IN CHARGE...
OF THE AVENGERS!

chapter 3

After Iron Man, Cap, Hulk and Thor's ship disappeared into the sky, the first thing Sam did was send a message to the other Avengers, asking them to meet. Within minutes he walked into the Avengers Tower's briefing room to find them already waiting for him.

'Thanks for coming, everybody,' said Sam as he went to the head of the table. Looking around, he was proud to be on a team with each of these heroes.

There was Natasha Romanoff, the Black Widow, a **S.H.I.E.L.D.** master spy and specialist in infiltration. Next to her was Clint Barton, AKA Hawkeye, not just the best archer in the world but also well versed in several forms of combat.

Across from Hawkeye were the Twins—two young Avengers who had recently joined the team and who had incredible powers. Pietro Maximoff—**Quicksilver**—could move with superhuman speed, and his sister, Wanda Maximoff—the **Scarlet Witch**—could use magic powers to blast back enemies.

Rounding out the team was **Vision**, an android built with a digital intelligence so advanced that he was actually a form of artificial life. Vision had superhuman strength and superhuman reflexes, as well as the abilities to phase through solid walls, shoot powerful beams and repair himself when injured.

'What's the story, Sam? Why the emergency message?' asked Hawkeye.

Sam used **holo-display** to help get his teammates up to speed on the possible threat from space.

'So what will we need to do if Iron Man and the others find this Thanos guy?' asked the Scarlet Witch, nervously.

'We're just going to have to wait for news from the advanced team,' responded Falcon, 'but the Avengers have beaten Thanos before, so we know we can again.' Falcon cleared his throat after saying the villain's name. Thanos was feared by everyone, including this Avenger.

'Okay. We wait for information . . . What do we do in the meantime?' asked Widow.

Falcon had been expecting this question. This group of Avengers was looking to **HIM** for leadership. Everything had been happening so quickly that Falcon hadn't had time to put together a plan, but he was quick on his feet.

'I was thinking of something like this . . .' said Sam as he presented a rotating patrol schedule that gave every Avenger duties and also time in the training room, as well as time off.

'With the others out in space, there's more world for each of us to protect,' admitted Sam, 'but I know that if we work together, we can handle it.'

Quicksilver reviewed Sam's plan, highly pleased with his organisational skills. 'Yeah, I think we can do this,' he confirmed.

Even Vision was impressed: 'Your proposal operates at near-peak proficiency, Sam Wilson.' That was really high praise, coming from the android.

As the Avengers ended their meeting and headed off to take care of their various responsibilities, Falcon smiled. He was starting to feel good about this whole '**leadership**' thing. Maybe Cap was right: maybe he was a natural leader.

SCHEDULE

PATROL

SCARLET WITCH	14:00 HRS
BLACK WIDOW	14:00 HRS
QUICKSILVER	15:00 HRS
FALCON	16:00 HRS

TRAINING ROOM PRACTICE

BLACK WIDOW	9:00 HRS
HAWKEYE	11:00 HRS
QUICKSILVER	11:00 HRS
VISON	12:00 HRS
SCARLET WITCH	13:00 HRS

chapter 4

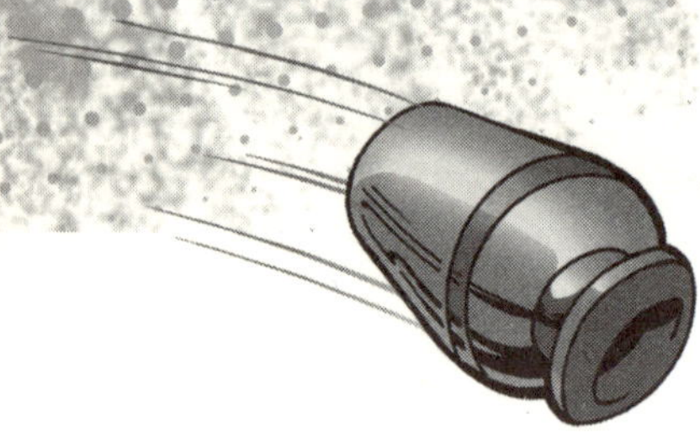

The next morning Sam woke to loud shouting coming from the common room.

He stumbled out of bed, throwing on his wing-pack. What could it be? Could villains have broken into the Avengers Tower? **Were they under attack?**

But it was nothing of the sort. Sam arrived to find Quicksilver and Hawkeye involved in a screaming match.

You better step back, archer. Don't forget you're talking to a hero with actual super powers, not just a bent stick with string on it.
Hero? HA, that's a laugh. I've helped save the world. You're just a newbie with an attitude.

'WHAT'S GOING ON HERE?'

Sam asked with genuine surprise as he stepped in between the two angry Avengers. Amid the shouted insults, Sam pieced the story together.

It turned out Sam's rotating schedule had them both using the training room that morning, and the two couldn't agree on which program to use, target practice or speed practice. The argument started small but quickly heated up to personal insults.

'Your practice schedule, that's what caused all this?' asked Falcon.

'I've got to keep up my skills,' said Hawkeye, waving his bow.

'You sure do. In fact, let's see how well you do without that thing,' said Quicksilver, zipping up at a blurring speed, yanking Hawkeye's bow away from him, and racing around the room with it.

'Hey, give me that!' shouted Hawkeye. 'I may not be able to keep up with you, but I can aim more than an arrow!' He started throwing vases, lamps and anything else he could get his hands on at Quicksilver.

'STOP IT,
BOTH
OF YOU!'

shouted Sam. **'You're behaving like children!'**

'Wait . . . Do you hear something?'asked Quicksilver.

Sure enough, they all heard more shouting coming from the hallway, but this time it was female voices. Within seconds the door slammed open and in came Black Widow and the Scarlet Witch, yelling at each other.

'Now what?' Sam asked them.

Like the schedule said they should be, both Black Widow and the Scarlet Witch were out on patrol when the gang of villains known as the **Wrecking Crew** were spotted battling a few police officers. Widow and Scarlet Witch both responded, trying to help. The only problem? They both went after the Wrecking Crew's leader, **Bulldozer.** The Scarlet Witch threw a hex at Bulldozer, but it missed and hit the nearby Widow instead.

The Wrecking Crew were eventually caught, but according to Widow, the situation could have turned out much worse.

'Wanda wasn't watching out for me,' Widow complained to Sam. 'I need teammates who have my back, not ones who shoot **at my back!**'

'It wasn't my fault!' shouted the Scarlet Witch. 'Widow jumped in where she wasn't needed and crossed my line of fire!'

'Where she "wasn't needed"?' asked Hawkeye incredulously.

'Black Widow's always needed in a fight,' he continued, clearly taking Widow's side.

'If my sister says it wasn't her fault, then it wasn't her fault,' shouted Quicksilver, sticking up for the Scarlet Witch.

Before long, Vision entered, watching the whole argument in confusion. It was clear that he didn't understand these very human conflicts.

Soon the argument turned into a four-way shouting fight, with Sam trying to calm everyone down—but he wasn't even able to make himself heard over everyone else!

Oh, man . . . What would Cap do in this situation? Sam asked himself.

But before he could figure it out, the Tower's alarm went off so loudly that everyone stopped and turned to check the wall screen.

'What's the situation, Jarvis?' Sam asked the computer.

'I'm afraid it's a red alert, sir,' reported the disembodied voice of Jarvis. **'Ultron is using his robot troops to attack somewhere in the city!'**

Ultron? The evil robot bent on destroying all of mankind? Oh, great . . .

chapter 5

'Avengers . . . assemble!' shouted Falcon as he, Black Widow, Hawkeye, Quicksilver, the Scarlet Witch and Vision gathered in front of **Horizon Labs.** He'd always wanted to be the one to shout that famous Avengers catchphrase, but under these circumstances it just wasn't as cool as he'd hoped it'd be.

'**Scans are useless**,' reported Vision as he attempted to use his enhanced eyesight to see inside the building. 'There's something blocking me.'

'Well, I guess we know where they went in,' said Hawkeye, checking out a massive breach in the side of the building.

'But that's not how they're going to come out,' shouted Quicksilver as he slipped towards the building at super speed.

'**Quicksilver, wait!**' Falcon shouted after the fleet-footed Avenger, but it was too late. Moving at almost the speed of sound, Quicksilver was already inside the building.

'Doesn't your brother know not to run off on his own during a team mission?' Black Widow demanded of the Scarlet Witch.

'If he were a **S.H.I.E.L.D.** agent, he'd be brought up on charges for taking off like that while under orders.'

'Don't start quoting **S.H.I.E.L.D.** regulations to me,' the Scarlet Witch said, bristling. 'Where we grew up there were no "rules of engagement" . . . there was only survival.'

Black Widow took a step towards Scarlet Witch, but before she could argue, Falcon stepped between the two.

'**Avengers!** Stop focusing on each other! The real enemy is inside, and he's not–' But before Falcon could finish, there was a loud crash, followed by Quicksilver's body flying through one of the lab's front windows and landing hard on the pavement at their feet.

'Pietro! Are you okay?' shouted the Scarlet Witch as she dropped to her brother's side.

'He is okay but unconscious,' reported Vision, scanning Quicksilver's body.

Suddenly a hail of laser-fire from inside the building sprayed around the Avengers, causing all the heroes to scatter and dive for cover.

Out of the building burst a half dozen identical Ultron units, robot soldiers that Ultron controlled and operated by remote.

'Ah, humanity's so-called heroes . . . How pathetic,' laughed Ultron as he emerged from the building behind his troops. With him were a few more units, all carrying boxes marked **'Vibranium'.**

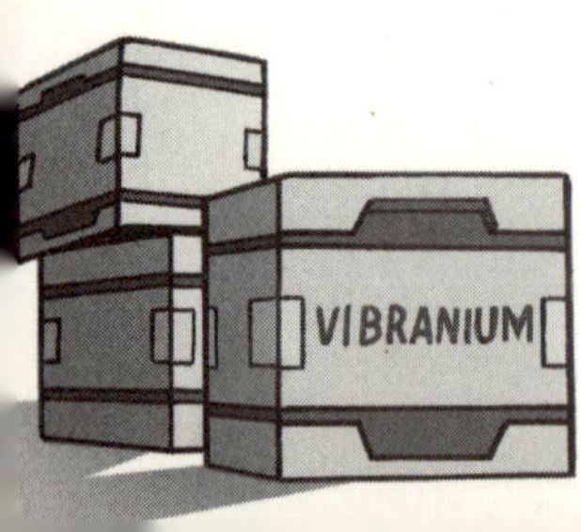

Ultron continued his rant. 'Don't you know by now that humanity is long since outdated? An update is coming!'

As soon as Falcon saw the boxes of Vibranium, he realised Ultron's plan. Vibranium was an extremely rare metal found in the African nation of **Wakanda.** Cap's shield was mostly made out of Vibranium, and the metal was able to absorb any vibrations or energy directed at it. If Ultron managed to coat his robot army with a skin of this rare metal, it would be practically indestructible. Nothing could stop it from marching across the face of the country, and eventually the world!

'Avengers, we can't let Ultron get away with those boxes,' shouted Falcon to the other heroes.

'Time to get on the defensive!'

Following Falcon's lead, the Avengers jumped into action. Widow **bounced** and **leapt,** getting behind the line of Ultron units, and unleashed **intense** fire from her wrist-mounted stinger weapons.

Nearby, Hawkeye fired off a series of **trick arrows**—explosive arrows, net arrows, oil-slick arrows—throwing everything he had at the robots!

At the same time, Vision confronted one of the troops, wrestling it and blasting it with his eye blasts.

Falcon took to the air, swooping in and firing from above. His manoeuvres drew the attention of a few of the troops, letting the

Scarlet Witch get close to Ultron unchallenged, where she loosed magical fire that burst around the maniacal villain!

I think we got this, Falcon thought, watching his team take down the bad guys and realising that Cap would be proud of them.

But seconds later, everything went wrong!

Hawkeye, having just brought down two of Ultron's robot troops, turned and fired an ice arrow at Ultron. At the same moment, one of the Scarlet Witch's beams blasted across the field of fire, bouncing Hawkeye's arrow back towards him!

Seeing this, Widow jumped forwards, attempting to shoot the arrow out of the sky, but instead she fired too soon and hit the Scarlet Witch.

The Scarlet Witch shouted in pain and fell to the ground. Vision broke off from his fight to run to the Scarlet Witch's side.

At that moment, Hawkeye's ricocheting arrow came right at him and popped, covering him with an instant-freeze fluid that encased him in a hard shell of ice!

'**Excellent!**' shouted Ultron as he grabbed the frozen Hawkeye and lifted him up. 'You bumbling excuses for Avengers do my work for me. This Avenger is an added prize that I didn't expect to win! Thank you, all.'

Ultron and the robot units carrying the Vibranium suddenly blasted into the sky with boot-jets. Falcon tried to fly after them, but there were too many units firing at him, and he was forced to break off the chase.

Within seconds Ultron was gone . . . and he had both a cache of indestructible metal and one of their teammates with him.

HAWKEYE!

chapter 6

Back at the Tower, the customary mission '**debriefing**' quickly became another shouting match. Black Widow yelled at the Scarlet Witch for deflecting Hawkeye's arrow back in his direction, and the Scarlet Witch yelled at Widow for hitting her with stings.

'Did you do that on purpose?' the Scarlet Witch demanded of Widow. 'I accidentally hit you when we were fighting the Wrecking Crew, and so you thought you'd pay me back or something?'

'Of course not,' responded Widow, offended. 'I was acting quickly to try to fix your mistake by blowing that arrow out of the air!'

Even Quicksilver and Vision had a heated exchange, or at least as heated as Vision ever got. Quicksilver declared that Vision should have been able to see inside the building, making it unnecessary for Quicksilver to run inside, but Vision pointed out that no-one ordered Quicksilver to run inside blind—he'd done it on his own.

'Protocol dictates awaiting approval before entering an enemy site,' Vision pointed out.

Quicksilver just rolled his eyes at Vision. '**Pfft . . . protocol . . .**'

Sam tried to control the discussion, but getting anyone's attention in all the fuss seemed to be impossible. Finally, he shouted at the top of his lungs:

Suddenly quieted, everyone turned and looked towards Sam in total surprise. Sam never shouted like that.

'There's only one person to blame for what happened today,' said Sam before pausing. Everyone leaned in, interested to see which side of the argument their temporary leader would come down on.

'The person to blame . . . is me. With more guidance and better leadership, you all would have won that battle . . . and Hawkeye would be safe.'

Sam felt like everything would have been different if Cap were there on Earth leading them, instead of on that space mission.

What would Cap have done differently? he thought. Sam didn't know, but he did know that Cap hardly ever made mistakes. In fact, maybe Cap's only mistake was leaving me in charge, he thought.

After Sam's statement, everyone felt awkward. They didn't continue the argument, but they didn't resolve it, either.

'I guess it doesn't matter whose fault it was,' said Widow. 'Either way Hawkeye is gone . . . **and I'm going to find a way to bring him back.**'

'Right,' said Quicksilver. 'When do we head out to look for him? I could race around the state in a grid pattern and–'

'Not "we", just me,' interrupted Widow. 'Hawkeye's my old partner from **S.H.I.E.L.D.**, and he's my responsibility. I'm used to doing operations on my own. I don't need anyone from this team to get in my way . . . or to shoot me in the back,' she finished, looking right at the Scarlet Witch.

Before anyone could reply, Widow turned on her heel and stormed out of the room. Everyone else looked back at Sam.

'She can just do that? Go off on her own like that?' asked Quicksilver.

'This isn't the military, this is the Avengers. She can do whatever she wants,' replied Sam.

'But . . . what do we do? Should we just let her go?' asked the Scarlet Witch.

Sam looked back at them. This was what it meant to be the leader. The team asked questions, and Sam had to be prepared to answer them. It was what Cap was counting on him to do . . .

But Sam didn't have an answer ready. What would Cap do if one of his teammates had been kidnapped and another one was planning on going solo to get him back?

After a pause, Sam spoke again.

'I–I don't know what we should do,' he admitted. It wasn't a very good answer, but it was the **truth.** 'Just give me some time to think,' said Sam, and then he, too, left the room.

The Twins, shocked, looked at each other in confusion. Vision, on the other hand, just watched Sam leave, a look of concern on his face.

chapter 7

Sam took the elevator straight to the roof of the Avengers Tower, extended his Falcon wings, and jumped off the edge. New York City looked so beautiful from above, glass from skyscrapers glinting in the sun like jewels.

But Sam couldn't enjoy the view knowing that somewhere there was an evil robot villain holding an Avenger hostage—a friend.

Even if he knew where Ultron was, even if he knew how to stop him, he couldn't. If his team wouldn't listen to him, how could he lead them into a dangerous mission? More Avengers could be kidnapped . . . **or worse!**

Before long Sam found himself landing at his favourite thinking spot, a perch on the top of the **Empire State Building.**

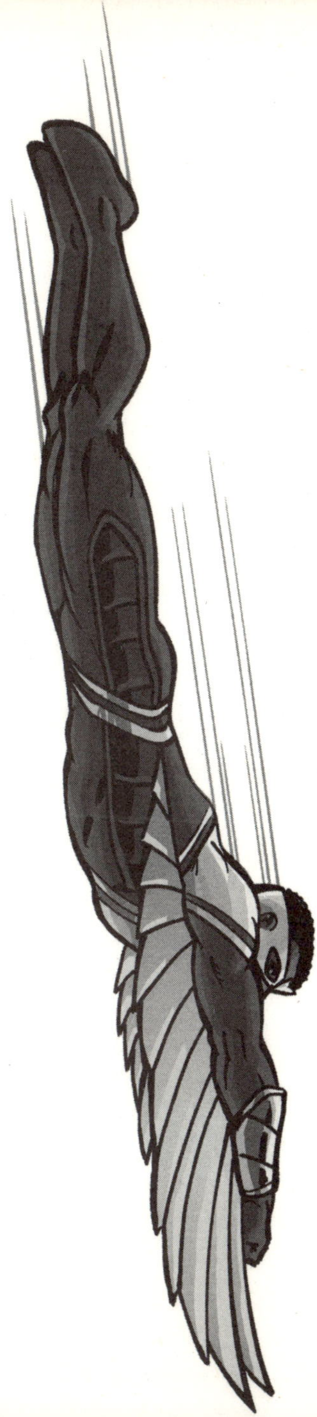

There he sat, looking out into space, imagining what Cap would say if he knew how badly Sam's first attempt at leadership had gone.

'I hope I am not disturbing you,' said Vision as he suddenly phased through the wall behind Sam.

'Augh!' shouted Sam in surprise. Vision's ability to pass through solid objects could be downright spooky! 'You scared me half to death.'

'Apologies, Sam Wilson,' said Vision. **'I came to offer you one cent in exchange for your ideas.'**

'The phrase is "a penny for your thoughts",' Sam said, correcting the android.

'Did I not just express that same meaning?' asked Vision.

'Yes, I suppose the words you used meant the

same thing'—Sam shrugged—'but it's a saying, and the saying is "A penny for your thoughts".'

'There is much about human communication that I still do not understand,' admitted Vision.

'Well . . . that's true of me, too, I guess,' Sam admitted, 'judging by what happened today.'

'I wanted to ask you about that,' said Vision. 'The Avengers are all on the same side, yet they seem to be caught up in non-productive verbal disputes. Why do they not get along?'

'Yeah, that's just humans,' explained Sam. 'Most of us want to get along with others, but sometimes personalities just clash. That's why a team needs a good leader to bring them together. If I were a better leader, like Cap, we wouldn't be having this problem.'

'Why did Captain America put you in charge of

the team if you are incapable of being a good leader?' asked Vision.

'I was just asking myself that,' admitted Falcon. 'Cap is a natural leader, so maybe he just thought he saw the same thing in me . . . But he was wrong. I don't always know what to do, like Cap.'

'Correction: Captain America didn't always know what to do,' stated Vision.

'Yes, he did,' said Falcon. **'Hello . . . that's why he's Cap!'**

'I'm sorry to contradict you, Sam Wilson, but I have all of Captain Steve Rogers' military records, and I can demonstrate to you that your statement is false . . .'

With that, Vision raised his palm and projected a hologram of a slightly younger-looking Captain America.

Sam leaned in and looked closely, focusing all of his attention as the hologram started talking.

'War journal, day forty-three:

We're trapped behind enemy lines, and I just don't know what to do . . .'

chapter 8

It was 1943, and Captain America was leading his elite team of soldiers, known as the **Howling Commandos**, on a raid deep into enemy territory when their plane was spotted and shelled down by **HYDRA** anti-aircraft weapons.

Miraculously, **Dum Dum Dugan**, one of the Howling Commandos, was able to bring the plane in for a crash landing, but it was way more 'crash' than it was 'landing'.

The commandos barely survived. All of them were injured in some way, ranging from cuts and scrapes to broken bones.

'We're behind enemy lines, near a HYDRA installation, and some of us are too injured to travel,' reported Cap in his private war journal. **'This is one of my first missions as team leader, and everyone is asking me what to do . . .**

'To be honest, I'm not sure what to tell them. Should we attempt to make it back to our base on foot?

'Or will that make us too much of a target? Maybe we should just dig in here, hide and wait for a rescue mission.'

Cap's next journal entry was even more dire. Some of the Howling Commandos, not getting any direction from Cap, were thinking about striking out on their own. Others refused to travel. It was getting more desperate by the minute.

'I'm filled with doubts,' Cap admitted to his war journal. **'I thought that I was ready to lead this team, but maybe I'm not. Maybe I'm just not cut out to be a leader at all.'**

But in his darkest moment, Cap found a picture of himself with Dr. Abraham Erskine and Howard Stark, the two brilliant scientists who had created the Super-Soldier process that gave Cap his special abilities.

'Looking at that photo gave me hope,' reported Cap. **'If those two great men believed in me enough to trust me, then I must be able to do the things they need me to do.'**

With determination, Cap searched for a solution. While checking the map, he realised that the nearby **HYDRA** base held fighter planes.

The Commandos might be too injured to make it all the way back to home base on foot, but he knew they could make it as far as the **HYDRA** base.

The Commandos who were less injured helped move the more seriously injured ones, and in a daring mission, they snuck into the **HYDRA** base, stole a plane, and flew it back to safety!

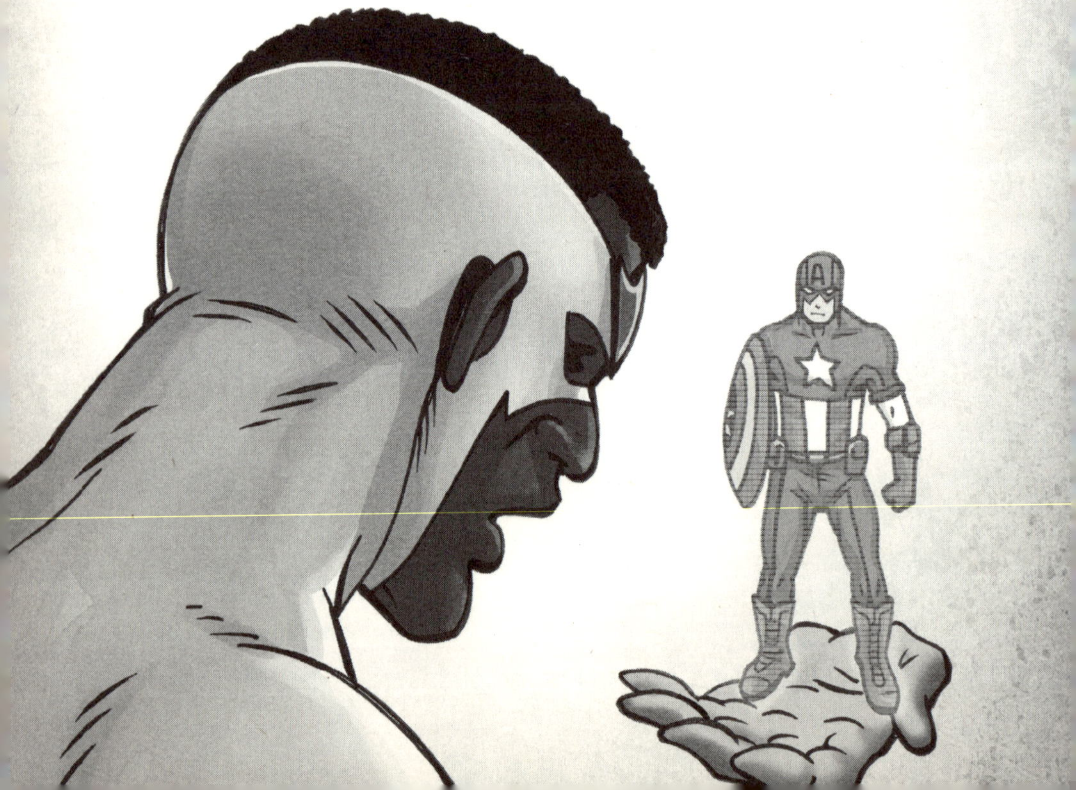

That experience led Cap to an important conclusion. **Half of leadership, he realised, was about believing in yourself and believing in your team.**

As Vision's hologram ended, Sam was surprised. 'Cap had to **learn** to be a leader?' he asked. 'I always assumed that he was a natural leader.'

Vision considered this. 'Maybe even a natural leader sometimes has difficult moments. Maybe what makes them "naturals" is that they never give up trying, even when they most want to.'

Falcon realised that Vision was right.

'**Come on, Vision, we've got to go**,' he said, extending his wings.

'Where are we going?' asked the android.

'Back to the Avengers Tower. I've got a team to lead.'

Sam got back to the Avengers Tower just as Black Widow was heading out on her solo attempt to locate and free Hawkeye. Quicksilver and the Scarlet Witch were quietly watching her go, not sure whether they wanted her to stay or not.

'**Wait**,' said Sam as he and Vision entered. 'You're not going anywhere.'

Widow spun around to face Sam, looking angry. 'Who's going to stop me? You? I'm not sitting around here. I'm going after Clint.'

'Yes, you are going after him,' said Sam. '**We all are. And we're doing it as a team!**'

This took everyone by surprise.

'Look,' said Sam, now with the room's full attention. 'I know I haven't been the best leader so far. But the Avengers were originally formed because there came a day, unlike any other, when Earth's Mightiest Heroes found themselves united against a common threat . . . and today, Ultron is that kind of threat.

'If the team were to split apart now, Ultron would be halfway to victory,' Sam pointed out. 'So far our team has been focusing on the things that separate us, but now it's time to focus on what unites us: our duty to the planet!'

Everyone looked around the room, realising that Sam was right. They nodded in agreement at each other.

'Okay,' said Widow. '**But how do we find Ultron?**'

Sam smiled.

'That's where my latest invention is going to come in handy,' he said with a grin. '**Follow me . . .**'

chapter 9

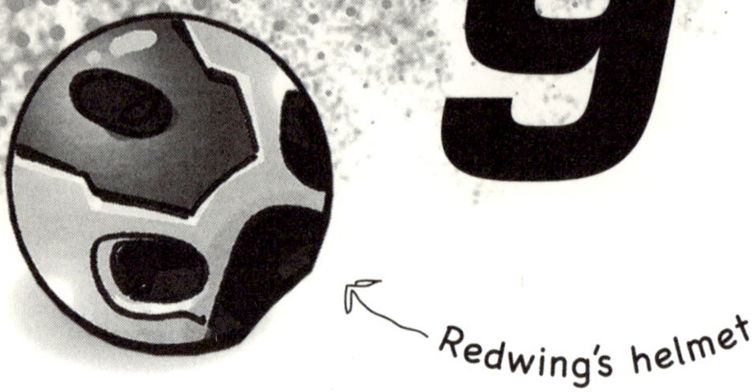

'A little small for you, isn't it?' asked Widow, looking at the tiny helmet in Sam's hands. They were now in Iron Man's lab, and Sam was showing the rest of the team the invention he'd been working on for the past several months. The helmet was sleek and aerodynamic but had wires and electrodes running along the sides of it.

'It's not for me,' Sam replied with a smile as he led them to the roof.

'This is Redwing.' He opened a massive birdcage and brought out a beautiful bird, a wild falcon with flaming orange, almost red, plumage. 'I found him sick in Rio and nursed him back to health. I trained him.'

'**Your invention is headgear for a bird?**' asked Quicksilver, confused.

'Not just any headgear,' Sam replied. 'This helmet links me to Redwing. Everything Redwing sees gets transferred to the display in my visor.'

'**You turned your pet bird into a webcam?**' asked the Scarlet Witch.

'Not just a webcam,' pointed out Widow. 'A spy cam. Redwing would be perfect for covert intelligence gathering.'

'How can this help us locate Hawkeye?' asked Vision.

'It helps because it doesn't stop with just Redwing,' explained Falcon. 'Redwing acts as a transceiver, broadcasting what he sees, but he also acts as a receiver. Through him I can actually detect the neurological impulses of other birds within his range.'

'Meaning what, exactly?' asked the Scarlet Witch.

'Meaning when Redwing has this on, I can see everything that is seen by any bird for miles around,' said Sam.

'But there are thousands and thousands of birds in the city,' pointed out Quicksilver.

'All the better to hunt Ultron with,' remarked Widow.

'Basically, you're trying to get all the birds of New York to work together as a team?' asked the Scarlet Witch.

'That's right! This is my first test of the system,' said Sam as he fitted the little helmet on the obedient Redwing. '**Fly, Redwing!** Show me what you see.' Then Sam released the bird into the sky.

Instantly, inside Sam's visor a window popped open showing him a bird's-eye view of the city. 'Huh,' said Sam. 'I only have Redwing's transmission, not any other–'

But before he could finish his thought, thousands of new windows started popping open, showing him views from every single angle of Manhattan!

'It's working!' Sam shouted, pleased.

Within an hour, Sam's visor computer had sorted through the images from the birds and was searching for signs of Ultron. Soon after that, the computer flagged an image seen by a pigeon under a bridge in a warehouse district north of the city. In the shot Sam could clearly see some of Ultron's robots entering a supposedly abandoned building through a side door.

'**We've got him,**' Sam announced to the team.

Once they arrived at the building, Widow popped the lock, and the team snuck inside.

Sure enough, the members of Ultron's robot army were walking the corridors, but using stealth, the Avengers took out several of them without being seen and made their way to a darkened computer centre deep inside the building.

'Can you hack into these, Vision?' Sam asked as he pointed to the racks of computers. 'Any information you find could give us a clue about the best way to take Ultron down.'

'I can utilise any system,' said Vision as he raised his hand to one of the terminals. Soon he was downloading the data from Ultron's hard drives. 'This data requires your attention,' Vision said, pointing to some information on a screen.

Sam bent in closer and took a look. He couldn't believe it. 'According to this, there was no signal from space!'

'**What do you mean?**' asked the Scarlet Witch.

'Thanos isn't putting together an army in space. The evidence was all set up by Ultron!' explained Sam. '**Iron Man, Cap and the others are on a wild goose chase. There's nothing up there for them to find!**'

'That's right!' came a booming voice from outside the room. 'I knew that if I could trick the core Avengers into leaving the planet, Earth would be mine for the taking! After all, the inferior Avengers left behind could be easily beaten.'

With that, Ultron stepped into the room, surrounded by his robot troops.

'"Inferior"?' Sam looked at Ultron calmly, no fear in his eyes, and then turned to his team and said simply, **'Let's show Ultron who's inferior . . .**

Avengers: ASSEMBLE!'

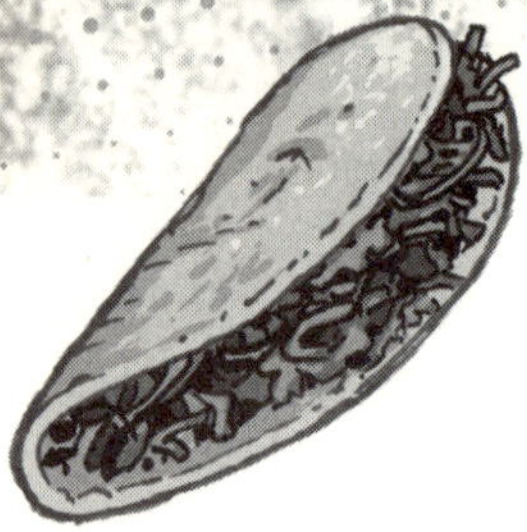

chapter 10

The fight was intense and brutal. Ultron's robots sprang on the Avengers, hacking, slashing and blasting like the remorseless machines of destruction they were designed to be!

But if Ultron was counting on the team being as disorganised as they'd been during the fight at Horizon Labs, he was sorely disappointed.

'Cover Vision,' directed Falcon, sending Widow, Quicksilver and the Scarlet Witch straight into combat. **'Vision, get Hawkeye's location from Ultron's computer.'**

Widow jumped, kicked and fired stings while the Scarlet Witch fell in behind her, shooting left and right, but being careful to always keep Widow in view.

At the same time, Quicksilver sped around Ultron himself, whipping up a whirlwind that prevented Ultron from even being able to shoot.

As soon as Vision got Hawkeye's location from the computer, Falcon called out a new plan of attack. He sent Vision to phase through Ultron's robots, smashing them, while the Scarlet Witch's magical hexes protected Black Widow's escape.

Widow made her way to Hawkeye and used her lock-picking skills to free the archer. Once Hawkeye was free, Sam ordered him to provide cover fire to support Quicksilver. With Hawkeye backing him, Quicksilver smashed robot after robot.

Soon all that was left was Ultron himself.

'This does not compute,' exclaimed Ultron. 'You are supposed to be the weak members of the Avengers . . .'

'A team is only as weak as its leader,' said Widow.

'And we've got a strong leader,' said Hawkeye, looking at Falcon. 'I can see that now.'

'Thanks, Hawkeye. Thanks, team.' Falcon smiled as he slashed his wing-blades across Ultron's circuits, shutting the maniacal robot down for good. They quickly called in **S.H.I.E.L.D.**, whose agents hauled Ultron off to a top-secret prison designed specifically for Super Villains of his calibre.

Later, the Quinjet zoomed past the moon towards Earth, ready to re-enter the atmosphere.

'**Hurry**,' Captain America urged Iron Man, who was in the pilot's seat. 'We need to get back and help the other Avengers!'

'I'm pushing this thing as fast as I can, Cap,' responded Iron Man.

Once they had reached the edge of the solar system and seen that there was no army out there, Cap, Iron Man, Hulk and Thor quickly realised that the signal had been faked. They didn't know who had done it, but they did know it meant that Falcon and the others were in trouble!

Soon the Quinjet docked at the Avengers Tower. Cap and the others rushed inside and were shocked by what they found:

The rest of the team was . . . **calmly hanging out, enjoying one another's company!**

Hawkeye was giving tips to Quicksilver on how to aim for the bullseye as they played darts.

On the other side of the room, the Scarlet Witch and Black Widow were having lunch together while talking about their favourite locations in Eastern Europe. It turned out they both had been to many of the same places.

Meanwhile, Sam was giving Vision a closer look at the helmet for Redwing. Vision was suitably impressed with the invention.

Everyone looked up as Cap and the others came running in. 'Sam, the signal from space, it was a–' started Cap.

But Sam finished Cap's sentence for him, saying, 'A trick. We know. Ultron did it. Don't worry, we took care of it.' Sam shrugged it off like it was no big deal. 'Hey, you guys hungry? We made tacos.'

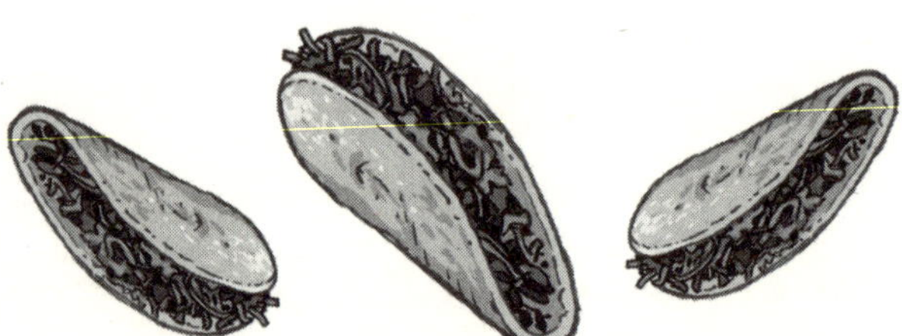

Cap and Iron Man looked at each other, relieved. Their concern had clearly been unnecessary. Falcon had it all taken care of.

'I like tacos,' said Iron Man.

That evening Cap was back in the Avengers training room, waiting patiently in the simulated redwood forest's treetops. Sam had asked to make another attempt at beating Cap in the 'capture the flag' training exercise, but it looked like Sam was going to lose again.

Cap saw Sam jump from the underbrush and head towards his flag, but Cap sprang into action. 'Sorry, Sam, not this time,' said Cap as he again tackled Sam in midair, taking him to the ground.

'I wouldn't be so sure about that,' said Sam, pointing up at the place where Cap's flag was hidden.

Cap looked up just in time to see Black Widow and the Scarlet Witch grabbing his flag and waving it around.

'**We did it!**' whooped the Scarlet Witch.

Cap was pleasantly surprised. No team had ever beaten him at capture the flag . . . until then. Good for them!

'It's like you said, Cap,' explained Falcon. 'This can be a leadership exercise, too.'

'That's true,' said Cap. 'I've said it once, and I'll say it again: Sam, **you're a natural leader.**'

Sam smiled. '**Yes, I am.**'